A
GENEALOGICAL ABSTRACT OF DESCENT
OF THE FAMILY OF
PIERREPONT
FROM
SIR HUGH DE PIERREPONT
OF PICARDY, FRANCE
A.D. 980

Old Motto: "Spes Tutissima Coelis."

COMPILED BY

Edward J. Marks

HERITAGE BOOKS
2011

HERITAGE BOOKS

AN IMPRINT OF HERITAGE BOOKS, INC.

Books, CDs, and more—Worldwide

For our listing of thousands of titles see our website
at
www.HeritageBooks.com

A Facsimile Reprint
Published 2011 by
HERITAGE BOOKS, INC.
Publishing Division
100 Railroad Ave. #104
Westminster, Maryland 21157

International Standard Book Numbers
Paperbound: 978-0-7884-3027-5
Clothbound: 978-0-7884-8798-9

TO

Mrs. Frances R. Martin,

OF

NEW HAVEN, CONN.,

THESE PAGES,

THE RESULT OF A LABORIOUS RESEARCH,

WHICH,

WITHOUT HER ENCOURAGEMENT AND AID WOULD

HAVE BEEN FRUITLESS,

ARE RESPECTFULLY INSCRIBED.

SECTION I.

THE FAMILY IN FRANCE AND ENGLAND.

A. D. 980—1564.

[The numerals indicate the different generations.]

I.

Sir Hugh de Pierrepont, A. D. 980, lord of "the Castle of Pierrepont in the south confines of Picardy, and diocese of Laon," a branch of the Pierreponts who were lords of Castle Pierrepont, two leagues from S. Saveur, Normandy, whence they derived their name.

The place derived its name from a stone bridge, with which Charlemagne supplied the place of a ferry. His son,

II.

Sir Godfrey Pierrepont,[1] succeeded and was father of Godfrey and Robert. Godfrey, son of Sir Godfrey, was father of Sir Ingolbrand, lord of Castle Pierrepont, Picardy, A. D. 1090, and ancestor of the French Pierreponts. The younger son,

III.

Sir Robert de Pierrepont,[2] Knight, came over from France to England as a commander in the army of William the Conqueror, 1066, from whom he received great estates in the counties of Suffolk and Sussex, among which was the lordship of Hurst Pierrepont. He was at the battle of Hastings with the conqueror, and by him ennobled for his conduct at that battle. His son,

IV.

William de Pierrepont,[3] second lord of the Manor of Hurst Pierrepont,[4] county Sussex. His son,

V.

Hugh de Pierrepont, living temp. Henry II. His son,

---

[1] "Hurst Pierrepont," by Ellis. [2] Universal Magazine, Nov., 1767, Bartow's Peerage, Burke's Extinct Peerage, Collins' Peerage, &c. [3] For particulars of the persons named in the line of descent, see the Peerage. [4] In the family records at Holme Pierrepont, the form, "Pierpont," was quite as frequent on old documents as "Pierrepont."

6

VI.

William de Pierrepont, had Simon, his successor, who died without issue. This William was of Holywell, in the county of Suffolk. He was succeeded by a younger son,

VII.

Robert de Pierrepont, who became sixth lord of the Manor of Hurst Pierrepont, in Sussex. His son was

VIII.

Sir Henry de Pierrepont, of Holbeck Woodhouse, in the county of Nottingham, Knight. (8 Edward I, 1280.) His son was

IX.

Sir Henry de Pierrepont, "a person of great note," fought in the battle of Lewes, 1264; died 1292. He married Annora, only daughter of Sir Michael de Manvers, lord of the Manor of Holme, of which he became possessed under the name of Holme Pierrepont,[1] county of Nottingham. This place is still in the family; the present proprietor being Sydney William Herbert Pierrepont, Earl Manvers, Viscount Newark, and Baron Pierrepont, of Holme Pierrepont.

Sir Henry was succeeded by his son Simon Pierrepont,—summoned a Baron to Parliament, June 8, (32 Edward I, 1304),—but died without issue. His younger son,

X.

Sir Robert de Pierrepont, of Holme Pierrepont, Knight, summoned a Baron to Parliament, temp. Edward 1; died 1333. His first wife was Sarah, daughter and at length heir of Sir John Herrize, of Wingfield, county of Derby, Knight. His second wife was Cecily, daughter of Anuesley, of Annesley, by whom he had issue: 1, Robert; 2, George; 3, Ralph; 4, John.

By his first wife he had issue, a daughter, Margaret, wife of Sir Gervase Clifton, Knight, and a son,

XI.

Sir Henry de Pierrepont,[2] of Holme Pierrepont, Knight, eldest son, married Margaret, daughter of William Fitz William, of

[1] For account of Holme Pierrepont and the Pierrepont family, see Thoroton's Nottingham. [2] For the information contained in the English line, the compiler is chiefly indebted to Earl Manvers, of Thoresby, Notts, and to Rev. Evelyn Bartow, of Baltimore.

Elmely, Knight, by Maude, only daughter of Edmund, Baron Deincourt. Sir William was a grandson of Thomas Fitz William, the son of Sir William Fitz William and Ella Plantagenet. They had Henry, who died without issue, and a younger son,

XII.

Sir Edmund de Pierrepont, maternally descended from the Kings of France and England, Counts of Normandy, Flanders and Anjou, and sixth proprietor of Holme Pierrepont, died at Gascoigne, France, 1370, having married Joan, daughter of Sir George Montboucher, of Gomulston, Notts, Knight, and was succeeded by his son,

XIII.

Sir Edmund Pierrepont, of Holme Pierrepont, Knight, living 1 Henry VI, 1423. Married Frances, daughter and co-heir of Sir William Franke, of Grimsby, county of Lincoln, Knight.

XIV.

Sir Henry Pierrepont, of Holme Pierrepont, Knight, living 19 Henry VI, died before 31 Henry VI, A. D. 1453. Married Ellen, daughter of Sir Nicholas Langford, Knight, a widow in 31 Henry VI, A. D. 1453. By her he had

1. Henry Pierrepont, eldest son, died young. Afterwards,

2. Henry Pierrepont, of Holme Pierrepont, Esq., Sheriff of Nottingham and Derby, 8 Edward IV, 1453, married Thomasin, daughter of Sir John Melton, of Melton Hall, county Derby, Knight, by whom he had Sir Henry Pierrepont, Knight, eldest son, and his successor, whose will was proved Dec. 18, 1499, and who married a daughter of Hugh Hastings, of Fenwick, in Cornwall, Ebor. He died without issue, and was succeeded by his younger brother,

XV.

3. Francis Pierrepont, of Holme Pierrepont, Esq., who died Nov. 9, 1495. He married Margaret, daughter of —— Pierrepont, of Langford, and had

First—An elder son, who died without issue, and

XVI.

Second—Sir William Pierrepont, of Holme Pierrepont, Knight Baronet. His first wife was Joan, daughter of Sir Richard

Empson, Knight, Chancellor of the Duchy of Lancaster, by whom he had issue,

1. Sir George Pierrepont, mentioned below, and
2. Thomas Pierrepont.

His second wife was Anne, daughter of Sir Brian Stapleton, of Carleton, in the county of York, by whom he had issue,

3. Edmund, married a sister of Sir John Heron, and died without issue.
4. Frances Pierrepont died without issue.
5. John Pierrepont.
6. Elizabeth; first, wife of Sir John Sacheverell, of Morley, Esq.; second, of Edward Ferrers, Esq.

XVII.

Sir George Pierrepont, eldest son, of Holme Pierrepont, Knight, was lord of several Manors in Nottingham and Derby, and one of the Knights of the Carpet that were made at the coronation of Edward VI, Feb. 22, 1547. He died March 21, 1564.

His first wife was Elizabeth, daughter of Sir Anthony Babbington, of Dethick, county of Derby, Knight. She died Nov. 9, 1543. Buried at Malling, in Kent. By her he had issue, Amor, wife of John Rossell, of Ratcliffe, Notts.

His second wife was Winnifred, daughter and heir of William Twaits, county of Norfolk, Esq. (After Sir George's death she married Sir Gervase Clifton, Knight, of Clifton, county of Nottingham.) By her Sir George Pierrepont had issue, three sons, viz. :

1. Henry, the ancestor of the Earls and Dukes of Kingston.
2. Gervase, died without issue.
3. William, believed to be the ancestor of the American branch, which is the representative line now (1880,) and two daughters, viz.:
4. Anne, unmarried, and a minor in 1564. She was, first, wife of Thomas Thorold; second, of Francis Beaumont, of Grace Dieu, county of Leicester, Esq. She was the mother of Francis Beaumont, the celebrated dramatic poet.
5. Isabel, wife of Sir John Harpen, of Swarkeston, county of Derby, Knight.

SECTION II.

THE KINGSTON PIERREPONTS.

1564—1773.

Sir Henry Pierrepont, of Holme Pierrepont, Knight, living in 1614, married Frances, daughter of Sir William Cavendish, of Chatsworth, in the county of Derby, and had issue,

XIX.

1. Robert Pierrepont, Lieutenant General of the forces under Charles I, born Aug. 6, 1584. Created (by Patent dated June 29, 3 Car., 1 Anno, 1627,) Baron Pierrepont, of Holme Pierrepont, and Viscount Newark, and July 25, 4 Car., 1 Anno, 1628, Earl of Kingston-upon-Hull, *both* to the *heirs male* of his body. Killed at Gainsborough, July 3, 1643, on the part of the King, and was buried at Cuckney, in the county of Nottingham. Married Gertrude, one of the two daughters and co-heirs of Henry Talbot, a younger son of George, Earl of Shrewsbury, born Sept. 29, 1580, died 1649.

   Besides Robert, first Earl of Kingston, Sir Henry had also the following named children:

2. Frances, wife of Thomas, Earl of Kelly, in Scotland.
3. Mary, wife of Fulke Cartwright, of Ossington, county Nottingham, Esq.
4. Elizabeth, wife of Richard Stapleton.
5. Grace, wife of Sir George Manvers, of Haddon,[1] county Derby, Knight.

Issue of Robert, first Earl of Kingston:

XX.

1. Henry Pierrepont, first son; baptized at Mansfield, county of Nottingham, April, 1607. Succeeded his father as

---

[1] "I once saw at Haddon Hall, in a window of its large hall, in stained glass, a copy of the arms of the Pierreponts."—H. E. Pierrepont, 1 Pierrepont Place, Brooklyn March 17, 1881.

Earl of Kingston in 1643. Created Marquis of Dorchester, March 25, 1645. Died Dec. 1, 1680. Buried at Holme Pierrepont.

His first wife was Cecilia, eldest daughter of Paul Bayning, Viscount Bayning, of Sudbury, and at length co-heir to her brother. Died at Twickenham, county Middlesex. Buried at Holme Pierrepont, Sept. 30, 1639. By her he had issue,

1. Anne, eldest daughter, baptized at St. Margarets, Westminster, March 9, 1630-1. Married John Manners, Lord Roos, only son of John, Earl of Rutland. Was divorced by act of Parliament, 1666.

2. Grace died unmarried, March 25, 1703, age 68. Buried in the Church of St. Anne, Westminster.

3. Robert. Baptized at St. Margarets, Westminster, March 17, 1631-2. Died without issue.

His second wife was Catherine, daughter of James Stanley, Earl of Derby. By her he had issue,

4. Henry, second son, died young.

5. Mary died young.

Other children of Robert, first Earl of Kingston:

2. Frances, eldest daughter, married Philip Rolleston, Esq. She died before her father.

3. Mary, born in Feb., 1619, died in infancy.

4. *William Pierrepont*, of Orton, county Hants, and in *Thoresby*, county Nottingham. Second son, age 6 in 1614, died Aug., 1687, buried at Holme Pierrepont.

Married Elizabeth, daughter and co-heir of Sir Thomas Harris, of Tong Castle, in the county of Salop, Baronet, Sergt. at Law. Died 1656. By her he had issue, five sons and five daughters, of whom

1. Robert Pierrepont, of St. Giles in the Fields, county Middlesex, Esq., was the eldest son, born Aug. 30, 1636; died in the lifetime of his father, 1669. His sons, Robert, (*see No. XXI*,) William and Evelyn, became respectively, third and fourth Earls of Kingston, and first Duke of Kingston. His daughter, Gertrude, born in 1661, married Lord Cheyne, Viscount New Haven.

2. Henry Pierrepont, second son, died unmarried, age 29, before 1673.
3. William Pierrepont, third son, died 1640, age 2.
4. George Pierrepont, fourth son, died unmarried, age 20, before 1673.
5. Gervase, fifth son, of Tong Castle, county Salop, 1688, created .Baron Pierrepont, of Ardglas, in Ireland, March 21, 1703, and Baron Pierrepont, of Harslope, county Bucks, Oct. 19, 1714. Died without issue, May 22, 1715, aged 66, *whereby his titles became extinct.*
   His wife was Lucy, daughter of Sir John Pelham, of Loughton, in the county of Sussex, Bart.
6. Frances, wife of Henry Cavendish, Earl of Ogle, and afterwards Earl, Marquis and Duke of Newcastle, Knight of the Garter. He died 1691.
7. Eleanor died young.
8. Margaret died young.
9. Grace married Gilbert Holles, Earl of Clare, Baron Houghton, of Houghton. He died Jan. 16, 1688, aged 55.
10. Gertrude, wife of George Montague, Viscount, and afterwards Marquis of Halifax.
5. Elizabeth, third daughter, born June, 1624, died 1696. Married by Gervase Pierrepont, her nephew.
6. Francis Pierrepont, of the town of Nottingham, Esq., third son, born in 1613, died Jan. 30, 1657, buried at Holme Pierrepont. His first wife was Elizabeth, daughter of Thomas Bray, of Eyham, county of Derby, Esq., by whom he had three sons and two daughters. His second wife was Alissimon, daughter of the Dean of York; *no issue.* Children by his first wife, Elizabeth:
   1. Robert, eldest son of Francis, of Nottingham, Esq., age 24 in 1662, buried Sept. 22, 1682, at Holme Pierrepont. His wife was Anne, daughter of Henry Murray, Esq., (Groom of the Bedchamber to King Charles I,) by Anne, Viscountess Bayning, his wife. She died Aug. 22, 1718, buried at Holme Pierrepont. Their children were:
      1. Francis Pierrepont, born March 10, 1661. Died

without issue, at Holme Pierrepont, Aug. 17, 1694.

2. George, second son, died an infant.

3. Jane, eldest daughter, wife of Bernard Gilpin, clerk.

4. Anne, second daughter, married Thomas New-port, Lord Torrington.

5. William Pierrepont, third son, aged 4 in 1764, buried at Holme Pierrepont, without issue surviving him. Robert had two sons by his second wife, (Elizabeth Darcy, daughter of Sir Thomas Darcy,) viz.:

6. William.

7. Samuel. Both died young.

2. William Pierrepont, second son, died an infant.

3. Henry Pierrepont, third son.

4. Elizabeth, living in 1651.

5. Frances died Oct. 23, 1681. Married William Paget, son and heir of William, Lord Paget.

7. Robert Pierrepont, fourth son, was living in 1639. Died, unmarried, in 1745.

8. George Pierrepont, of Old Cotes, in the county of Derby, Esq., sixth and youngest son of Robert Pierrepont, first Earl of Kingston, born in July, 1628, buried at Holme Pierrepont, July 7, 1666. Married Mary, daughter of Isaac Jones, of London, General, and sister of Sir Samuel Jones, of Courtenhall, county of Nottingham, Knight. By her he had issue:

1. Henry Pierrepont, of Old Cotes, county Derby, Esq., eldest son, died without issue.

2. Samuel Pierrepont, second son, died unmarried Sept. 1, 1707, buried at Statton, county Derby.

9. Gervase Pierrepont, fifth son, died without issue.

XXI.

Robert Pierrepont, eldest son of Robert Pierrepont, of St. Giles in the Fields, mentioned above as the eldest son of William Pierrepont, of Orton and Thoresby, who was the second son of Robert, first Earl of Kingston. Succeeded, on the death of his great uncle, Henry, Marquis of Dorchester, to the honors of Earl of Kingston, Viscount Newark, and Baron Pierrepont, of Holme Pierrepont. Died, unmarried, at Dieppe, France, in June, 1682.

William Pierrepont, brother of preceding, second son of Robert Pierrepont, of St. Giles in the Fields, succeeded his brother Robert as Earl of Kingston, &c.; aged 11 in 1673, died Sept. 17, 1690, without issue; buried at Holme Pierrepont. His wife was Jane, eldest daughter of Robert Greville, Lord Brooke, died without issue, buried at Holme Pierrepont, Sept. 23, 1702.

Evelyn Pierrepont, third son, aged 22 in 1687, succeeded his brother William as Earl of Kingston, &c., 1690. Created Marquis of Dorchester Dec. 23, 1706, with remainder to his uncle, Gervase, Lord Pierrepont. Created Duke of Kingston July 20, 1715, Lord Privy Seal, 1716, President of the Council, 1719. Elected Knight of the Garter April 29, 1719, installed June 24th following. Died March 5, 1725, buried at Holme Pierrepont.

His first wife was Mary, daughter of William and sister of Basil Fielding, Earl of Denbigh. Marriage license dated May 27, 1687; age 19; buried Dec. 20, 1692, at Holme Pierrepont. She was a second cousin of Henry Fielding, the celebrated humorist and author of "Tom Jones." By her he had issue:

1. Mary Pierrepont, eldest daughter, afterwards known to the world and English literature as Lady Mary Wortley Montague. She was born at Thoresby, in 1690, and was remarkable for her precocious ability and attainments.

   In 1712 she was married to Edward Wortley Montague, who in 1714 became one of the Lords of the Treasury. Lady Mary, on her first appearance at St. James, was hailed with universal admiration, as much for her conversation as her beauty. In 1716 she accompanied her husband to Constantinople, whither he was sent as Ambassador to the Port, and Consul General to the Levant.

   At Belgrade she first witnessed inoculation for the small pox, which in 1718 she applied to her two children, and on her return to England introduced it there. She lived some time at Twickenham, in close intimacy with Pope, and from 1739 to 1761 in Italy. Her letters descriptive of the court and society of Vienna, and the scenery and customs of the East were published surreptitiously after her death, (4 volumes, 1763-7.) The best edition of her letters and works is by her great grandson, Lord Whamcliffe. Dallway published an edition in 1803, the basis of which was the manuscript collection in the possession of her grandson, the Marquis of Bute. She was the *sevigne* of English literature. She had one son, Edward Wortley Montague, born 1713, died 1776. He was returned to Parliament in 1747, but soon became so involved in debt that he was obliged to resign. He went to Italy, where he became a Roman Catholic, and from Italy to Egypt, where he became a Mohammedan. His autobiography appeared in 1869. Lady Mary's daughter married the Earl of Bute, and became ancestress of the present Marquis of Bute, who was lately received into the Catholic church.

2. Frances, second daughter, married John Erskine, Earl of Marr, who was attainted for rebellion in favor of the Pretender, and was the organizer of "Marr's Rebellion."

3. Evelyn, third daughter, married John, Lord Gower, who was created Earl Gower.

XXII.

4. William Pierrepont, Esq., only son, commonly called Lord Kingston, born Oct. 21, 1692, died in the lifetime of his father, July 1, 1713, aged 21, buried at Holme Pierrepont. Married Rachel, daughter of Thomas Baynton, Esq., who died May 18, 1722, buried at Holme Pierrepont. He had issue:

1. Evelyn Pierrepont, mentioned below.

2. Frances Pierrepont, only daughter, married Philip Meadows, of Brook street, pariole of St. George, Hanover Square, county of Middlesex, deceased.

XXIII.

Evelyn Pierrepont, only son of William, heir to his grandfather in the honors of Duke of Kingston, &c., 1726, Master of the Staghounds, 1738, elected Knight of the Garter March 20, 1740-1, installed April 21st following. Lord of the Bedchamber, Major General in the army, 1755, Lieutenant General, Lord Warden of the Forest of Sherwood, and Custos Rotutorum of the county of Nottingham. Appointed a General, May, 1772, chosen Recorder of Nottingham in December, 1768. Died, without issue, at Bath, Sept. 23, 1773, aged 62, and was buried at

Holme Pierrepont, Oct. 19, 1773, whereupon the titles of Earl of Kingston, Viscount Newark, and Baron Pierrepont, as is generally believed, passed of right to James Pierrepont, of New Haven, Conn., eldest son of Rev. James Pierrepont, (*See American descent below, XXII.*) The American claimants have, however, never succeeded in establishing their rights in this respect.

NOTE.—Charles Meadows, second son of Frances Pierrepont, (the last Duke's sister,) and Philip Meadows, came into possession of the Pierrepont estates, as is alleged, *under his uncle Evelyn's will in 1773*. He was created Baron Pierrepont and Viscount Newark, in 1796, and Earl Manvers, in 1806. Died in 1816. He was succeeded by his second son, Charles Herbert, born in 1778, married in 1804, died in 1860, when the prsent Earl, Sydnew William Herbert Pierrepont, succeeded him. He has three sons and two daughters, one of the latter, Emily, being the wife of Earl Beauchampe.

SECTION III.

THE FAMILY IN ENGLAND AND AMERICA.

1564—1880.

William Pierrepont,[1] third son of Sir George Pierrepont, of Holme Pierrepont, who died March 21, 1564, leaving issue as above stated (in the English line.)

1. Sir Henry, of Holme Pierrepont, eldest son.
2. Gervase, who afterwards died without issue.
3. William, above named.

The Heralds College Record describes him as " William Pierrepont, third son, mentioned in the will of his father, 1564, of Brereton, county Chester. Elizabeth, his wife, executrix to his will," (1648.) By her he had five sons:

1. William Pierrepont, eldest son, mentioned in his father's will (male issue extinct.)
2. Richard Pierrepont, second son, mentioned in his father's will, 1648, was married and had issue, but no male issue in 1773, at the time of the death of Evelyn, second Duke of Kingston.
3. James Pierrepont, the first of the family who ever bore that name, third son, mentioned in his father's will, 1648.
4. Joseph Pierrepont, fourth son.
5. Joshua Pierrepont, of Witherington, in Cheshire, youngest son, mentioned in his father's will, 1648. The descent for four generations (to 1788) from this youngest son, Joshua, is carefully recorded in the Heralds College, with what object in view is conjectural, but such conjectures point to the probability of the record being made in 1773–1780, when the question of the American claimants was under consideration. The descendants of Joseph, as given by the Heralds College, are as follows (substantially):

---

[1] Hollister's History of Connecticut, i, 459. Barlow Genealogy, 193.

19th Generation—Joshua Pierrepout, married Ann Yerwood, and had issue.

20th Generation—John Pierrepont, of Hough, parish of Wilmslow, county of Chester, baptized at Sweltenham, March 14, 1660, died 1743, buried at Wilmslow. Married Elizabeth Holton, and had issue.

21st Generation—William Drummond Pierrepont, of Chelsea, county of Middlesex, only son, a Captain in the Guards, born at Chorley, in Cheshire, 1691, died 1737, buried at St. Pancras, county of Middlesex. By his second wife had issue:

1. Hannah, married John Glover.
2. Mary, married Edward Whittaker.
3. Anne, married John Bell.

By his first wife he had issue:

22d Generation—John Pierrepont, of Cold Harbor, in Titherington, Cheshire, only son, born at Macclesfield, county of Cheshire, married Margaret, daughter of William Bancroft, of Macclesfield, at Prestbury, and had issue, ten children, viz.:

23d Generation:

1. Bancroft Pierrepont, of Kevidge, near Macclesfield, born in 1735, married Anne Broxer, of Bollington.
2. Mary, wife of James Brooke.
3. John Pierrepont, second son, unmarried, died at sea.
4. Anne Sophia, second daughter.
5. Hannah, third daughter.
6. William Pierrepont, third son, of Titherington, born at Macclesfield, 1739, living in 1788. First wife, Anne Ridgeway, of Titherington. Second wife, Mary Oldham, of Titherington.
7. Roger Pierrepont, fourth son, of the Broadway, Blackfriars, London, died 1780.
8. George Pierrepont, sixth son, died unmarried.
9. Joshua Pierrepont, of London, fifth son, died 1783.
10. James Pierrepont, of Bollington, Cheshire, afterwards of Charleston, South Carolina, America, seventh son.

XIX.

James Pierrepont,[1] from Holme Pierrepont, and second cousin to Robert Pierrepont, first Earl of Kingston. He was heir[2] to a large estate in Derbyshire, and carried on a trade between England and Ireland.

A letter written by his great grandson, James Pierrepont, Jan. 20, 1774, to Rev. Eleazar Wheelock, President of Dartmouth College, contains the following postscript[3]: "I am sorry that in my narrative I did not mention that my grandfather, John Pierpont, who first came into New England, was ye son of James Pierrepont who fell into trade with a partner between London and Ireland, but in the troublous[4] times they were bankrupt, which he hearing, sent for his brother Robert, and offered him part of his farm at Roxbury.[5] Accordingly he came, and they lived as brothers. They had three sisters at least; one was married to Mr. Eaton, minister of Bridport, who was silenced for dissenting from ye church of England.[6] James, after he failed, came over here to see his children, and died at Ipswich, in this country. I have heard that my grandfather had often presents sent to him by his friends in Derbyshire.

YR. JAMES PIERPONT.

Endorsed from Mr. James Pierpont, Jan. 20, 1774."

James Pierrepont, of London, died at Ipswich, Mass. A careful search of the tombstones at Ipswich, and of the record made of them some forty years ago, discloses no traces of his burial there. It is probable that he was buried at Roxbury, the residence of his sons John and Robert. By his wife, Margaret, who died in London, a widow in 1664, he had five children, viz. :

XX.

1. Hon. John Pierrepont, born in London, 1619, settled near Boston in 1640, leaving his father in London. In 1656 he purchased three hundred acres, now the site of Roxbury and Dorchester. Died Dec. 7, 1682, having been an influential citizen of Roxbury, and a Representative to the General Court. His grave is in

---

[1] Hollister's History of Connecticut, i, 459. [2] Bartow's Genealogy, p. 193. Savage's New England Settlers. [3] Communicated to the compiler by Dr. John Pierrepont C. Foster, of New Haven, Conn. [4] The Cromwellian Era. [5] Near Boston. The Dorchester precinct of Boston was named by this John Pierpont, after Henry Pierrepont, created Marquis of Dorchester in 1645. [6] Bartow Genealogy, p. 193. Family paper, in possession of H. E. Pierrepont, Esq., Brooklyn, N. Y.

the old burying ground at Roxbury, and remains in tolerably good preservation to this day.

2. Robert Pierrepont, born in London in 1621, married Sarah ——. In the manuscript account of the early inhabitants of Ipswich, by Abraham Hammett, occurs the following: "Pearpoynte, Robert, was a subscriber to Major Denison's allowance in 1648;" also "John Pierpont purchased of Wm. Fellows, Nov. 15, 1649, fifteen acres of land butting upon the land of John Brown on the south, and upon the land of Thomas Howlett on the west, upon the great brook toward the north."

Farmer, on the authority of "Sarah Pierpont's deposition," 1724, says, "James Pierpont came from England and died at Ipswich, leaving two sons, John and Robert."

Robert Pierrepont died at Roxbury, but in what year is unknown. His great grandson, Robert, went to Calais and St. Petersburgh under the patronage of his "kinswoman," the (soi disant) Duchess of Kingston.

3. Mary Pierrepout, born in Ireland.
4. Anne Pierrepont.
5. Martha Pierrepont, married Rev. William Eaton, vicar of Bridport, county Dorset.

By thankful Stow, his wife, Hon. John Pierrepont had the following issue:

1. John Pierpont, (as the family began now to write their name,) born 1652, died without issue, 1690.

XXI.

2. James Pierpont, born at Roxbury, Jan. 4, 1659, graduated at Harvard College, 1681, settled in New Haven, Conn., as pastor of the First Congregational Church, 1684. Took possession of the Mansion House and land granted him by the town, 1686. He died Nov. 22, 1714, and is buried under the Center Church in New Haven. He was pastor of the First Church for thirty years, and was one of the founders of Yale College, over which two of his descendents, Timothy Dwight, and Theodore Dwight Woolsey, have presided. He married, first, Abigail Davenport, Oct.

27, 1691, who died Feb. 3, 1692, childless. Married, second, May 30, 1694, Sarah, granddaughter of Governor Haynes, who died Oct. 27, 1696, leaving one child, Abigail, wife of Joseph Noyes. Married, third, July 26, 1698, Mary Hooker, granddaughter of Rev. Thomas Hooker, of Marsfield, county Leicester, England, afterwards the first minister (settled,) of Hartford, Conn. Original portraits, (painted in 1711,) of Rev. James Pierpont, and Mary, his wife, are now in the possession of their descendants, the Misses Foster, in the John Pierrepont mansion, (built in 1767,) in New Haven.

3. Ebenezer Pierrepont, born 1660, married Mary Ruggles, of Roxbury, died 1696. Left issue:

   1. John.

His son John went several times to London, where he died. He visited his kinsman, the Duke of Kingston, and was courteously entertained.

   2. Ebenezer.
   3. Mary.
   4. Joseph Pierrepont, born 1666, died without issue.
   5. Benjamin Pierrepont, born 1668, died without issue, at Charleston, S. C., 1680.
   6. Experience Pierrepont, born 1654.

Children of Rev. James Pierrepont, and Mary, his third wife:

XXII.

1. James Pierrepont, born at New Haven, Conn., May 21, 1699. He was educated at Saybrook College, (the nucleus of Yale,) and was tutor in Yale from 1722 to 1724. In early life he married and settled in Boston, afterwards returned to New Haven, and with his family occupied his father's residence. He was instrumental in forming the White Haven Church in 1742, and contributed largely towards the "Blue Meeting House," (so called from its color,) situated on the south east corner of Elm and Church streets. Rev. George Whitfield was twice the guest of Mr. Pierrepont; in October, 1740, and again in 1745. On the latter occasion " he preached to an immense audience from a platform under the elm tree in front of

Mr. Pierrepont's house." Mr. Whitfield also visited, at Northampton, Mass., Sarah, sister of Mr. Pierrepont, and wife of President Edwards, senior. Mrs.. Edwards is described by contemporaries as "a beautiful, intelligent and accomplished lady, a rare example of early piety, and as a Christian and Christian mother as nearly a perfect model as is often seen on earth."

The original Pierrepont mansion (built in 1686 on part of the town plat which was assigned to Rev. James Pierrepont when he was settled in the ministry in New Haven) stood on the spot now (1880) occupied by Wm. B. Bristol, Esq., corner of Elm and Temple streets. James Pierrepont died June 18, 1776, at New Haven. His last days were rendered unhappy by his vain efforts to obtain his rightful honors and estates in England. He married, first, Sarah Brick, who died childless; second, Anna Sherman, who died in 1803.

2. Samuel Pierrepont, born Dec. 30, 1700, graduated at Yale, 1718, ordained Dec. 10, 1722, drowned March 15, 1724, in crossing the Connecticut river in a canoe with an Indian.

3. Mary Pierrepont, born 1703, married Rev. William Russell, of Middletown, Conn. Gen. Wm. H. Russell, of Wooster Square, New Haven, is a lineal descendant.

4. Joseph Pierrepont, born Oct. 21, 1704, married Hannah Russell, died 1748. Lived at North Haven, Conn. He had issue:

1. Samuel.
2. Joseph.
3. James.
4. Benjamin.
5. Giles.
6 Hezekiah.

Giles, the 5th son, born 1741, died 1832, aged 91. He had two sons and four daughters. His second son, Giles Pierrepont, born May 1, 1783, married Miss Munson, of New Haven, and had one son, . Munson Pierrepont, afterwards known as Edwards

Pierrepont. He was born Nov. 4, 1813. In 1878–9
he was the American Minister to the Court of St.
James.

5. Benjamin Pierrepont, born Oct. 15, 1707, graduated at
Yale in 1726, died 1737, in the West Indies, unmarried.

6. Sarah Pierrepont, born Jan. 9, 1710, married July 28,
1728, Rev. Jonathan Edwards, President of Prince-
ton College, author of "The Freedom of the Will,"
and other metaphysical works, which have received
the highest enconium from European scholars. They
had three sons and eight daughters. Their daughter
Mary married Timothy Dwight, whose son, Rev.
Timothy Dwight, was President of Yale College from
1795 to 1817. Their daughter Esther married Rev.
Aaron Burr, whose son, Aaron Burr, afterwards became Vice-President of the United States. This Aaron
Burr married Theodosia Bartow, only child of Theo-
dosius Bartow, born in 1746, married, first, in 1765,
Col. Frederick Prevost, a near relative of Lt. Gen.
Sir George Prevost, Baronet, of Belmont, county
Hants, and Governor General in North America.
Col. Prevost dying in the West Indies in 1779, his
widow married, July 2, 1782, Col. Aaron Burr, and
had issue by him Theodosia Burr, only child, born
1786, married Joseph Alston, of South Carolina, by
whom she had an only child, a son, named Burr Alston. She was lost at sea with her child while going
from Charleston, S. C., to New York, to join her
father.[1]

7. Hezekiah Pierrepont,[2] youngest son of Rev. James Pierrepont, of New Haven, Conn., born at New Haven,
May 26, 1712, married Feb. 9, 1736, Lydia Hemenway, daughter of Rev. Jacob Hemenway, of East
Haven, died at New Haven, Sept. 29, 1741. His
children were:

---

[1] Harper's Magazine. Bartow's Genealogy, page 158. [2] Bartow's Genealogy, page
194. Hough's Lewis Co., 243. Hough's Franklin Co. Stiles' Brooklyn, II, 147. Dodd's
East Haven Register. For facts relative to descendants of Hezekiah Pierrepont, I am indebted to Henry C. Pierrepont, Brooklyn, N. Y., and Dr. John P. C. Foster, New Haven,
Conn.

1. Jacob Pierrepont, born 1738, died in the army at Crown Point, March, 1760.
2. John Pierrepont, born at New Haven, June 1, 1741, married Dec. 29, 1767, to Sarah Beers, daughter of Nathan Beers, of New Haven. She was born Oct. 29, 1744, died April 15, 1835, aged 90½. At the time of his marriage he moved into a new mansion, erected 1767, on land originally deeded by the town of New Haven to his grandfather, Rev. James Pierrepont, in 1685. As before stated, this building is now occupied by his grand children, and there is only one deed of conveyance between the present owners (1880) and the aboriginal Indians, from whom it was purchased over 250 years ago. A younger brother of Mrs. John Pierrepont, Nathan Beers, joined, April 21, 1775, the 2d Co. Governor's Guards, of which Benedict Arnold was Captain, and served until the end of the war, 1783. He commanded the company which guarded Major André the night before his execution, and was thanked by André for his considerate kindness to him on that occasion. The pen and ink sketch made at that time, by André, of his passage down the Hudson in a small boat to return to the British fleet, was presented by him to Nathan Beers, and is now in the possession of Yale College. Children of John and Sarah Beers Pierrepont.
(A.) Hezekiah Beers Pierrepont,[1] born at New Haven, Nov. 3, 1768, married Jan. 21, 1802, Anna Maria Constable, daughter of William Constable,[2] of New York. Lived in Brooklyn, on the heights. Died Aug. 11, 1838. Children, besides several who died young:
1. Hon. William C. Pierrepont, of Pierrepont Manor, New York. Born Oct. 3, 1803. Married June 2, 1830, Cornelia A. Butler,[3] (daughter of Benjamin Butler, of Oxford, New York.) Born at New York, March 1, 1806. Died Dec. 10, 1871.[4]

[1] Hough's Lewis Co. 243. Hough's Franklin Co. Stiles Brooklyn, 147. [2] For Constable Pedigree, see Barlow's Genealogy, page 197. [3] Hyde Genealogy. Walworth.

Her grandfather, Dr. Benjamin Butler, married Diadama Hyde. Born Dec. 10, 1740, who was the great-great-granddaughter of William Hyde, one of the first proprietors of Norwich, Conn., (1633,) while her grandmother, Jerusha Perkins, was the great-granddaughter of John Perkins, who came to Boston with Roger Williams, in 1631, and died June 29, 1700. Their children,

1. Robert Devereux, died unmarried in 1834.
2. Sarah Evelyn, married William Hull.
3. Emily J., married S. G. Wolcott, M. D.
4. Mary D., resides (1880,) at Pierrepont Manor.
5. Cornelia B., married G. H. Van Wagenen.
6. Anna M., married W. Mansfield White.
7. William D., died, (ætat. 17,) Sept. 5, 1863.

2. Anna C. Pierrepont, born 1805, married G. G. Van Wagenen.
3. Caroline Pierrepont, died unmarried.
4. Henry Evelyn Pierrepont, born Aug. 8, 1808, married Anna M. Jay, granddaughter of John Jay, 1st Chief Justice of the United States, minister to the Court of St. James, and author of Jay's Treaty. Resides No. 1 Pierrepont Place, Brooklyn, N. Y. Their children are:

1. Mary R. Pierrepont, born ——, 1842, married ——, 1863, to Rutherfurd Stuyvescent, a descendant of Petrus Stuyvescent, the last Dutch Director General of New York. She died Dec. 31, 1879, in New York City.
2. Henry E. Pierrepont, born Dec. 9, 1845, married Dec. 9, 1869, Ellen Low. Has issue:
    1. Anne L.
    2. Ellen L.
    3. Henry E.
    4. Robert L.
3. John Jay Pierrepont, born ——, 1849, married Elisé de Rham.
4. William A. Pierrepont, died 1879.
5. Julia J. Pierrepont.
6. Anna J. Pierrepont.

5. Emily C. married Joseph A. Perry, of Bay Ridge, L. I., A. D. 1834.
6. Frances M. married Rev. Frederick S. Wiley.
7. Harriet C.,[1] born July 17, 1818, married Edgar T. Bartow, Nov. 13, 1838, died July 6, 1855.
8. Mary Montague died, unmarried, 1853.
9. Maria T. married Joseph I. Bicknell, of Riverdale, N. Y.
10. Julia E. married John Constable, of Constables, N. Y.
11. Ellen Isaphene married Dr. J. M. Minor, of Fredericksburgh, Va. Died 1879.

(B.) Hannah Pierrepont, born 1776, married Claudius Herrick. Their children:
1. John Herrick, M. D., born 1805, married 1836, died Jan. 28, 1848. Left issue.
2. Edward Herrick, (Librarian of Yale College,) died unmarried.
3. Henry Herrick, born March 5, 1803, married Feb. 19, 1835. Has a family.

(C.) Mary Pierrepont, born April 3, 1778, married, first, Edward O'Brien, Nov. 11, 1796. Children by this marriage:
1. Henry O'Brien, born Oct. 15, 1797, died unmarried.
2. Eliza M. O'Brien, born Nov. 25, 179–, married Eli Blake of New Haven, July 18, 1822, died April 15, 1876.

Married, second, Eleazer Foster, Jan. 12, 1806. He was the the son of Edward and Rachael (Newell) Foster, born in Union, Conn. Graduated at Yale, in 1802, and was a prominent lawyer in New Haven, at the time of his death, in 1819. He was descended from Samuel Foster, who came from England, and settled in Wenham, Mass., and was made freeman of that place in 1650. He afterwards removed to Chelmsford, where he was chosen a representative in 1671. Died in 1702, aged 82. Children of Mary Pierrepont and Eleazer Foster:
1. Pierrepont B. Foster, born Sept. 8, 1809.
2. Eleazer K. Foster, born May 20, 1813, at New Haven.

---

[1] See Bartow Genealogy.

Graduated at Yale, in 1834; studied law partly in New Haven, and partly in the office of W. T. Worden, Esq., at Auburn, N. Y., was admitted to the bar in New Haven, in March, 1837, and resided there in the practice of his profession, until his death, June 13, 1877. He married Miss Mary Codrington, a lady of English birth, (cousin of General and Admiral Codrington, and of the Duchess of Beaufort), and formerly of Kingston, Jamaica, Jan. 2, 1838. Appointed Judge of Probate for the New Haven District, in the years 1845-6, 8-9. Represented the town of New Haven in General Assembly, in the years 1844, 1845, and 1865, when he was elected speaker of the House. Died June 13, 1877. Children of Eleazer and Mary (Codrington) Foster:

1. William E. (Yale graduate), editor, "Commercial Advertiser," Buffalo, N. Y.
2. Eleazer K., (Yale graduate), practicing law at Sanford, Florida.
3. John P. C. (Yale graduate), practicing physician, New Haven, Conn.

3. Edward W. Foster, born March 28, 1819. Has one son and one daughter.

4. Mary Anne Foster,
5. Harriet Foster,
6. Jane Foster,
7. Caroline Foster.
   } They occupy the "old Pierrepont House," on Elm St., New Haven, Conn.

(D.) John Pierrepont, born 1780, died unmarried, 1836.

(E.) Nathan Pierrepont, born 1782, died unmarried, 1803.

Children of James Pierrepont and Anna Sherman Pierrepont.

XXIII.

1. Evelyn Pierrepont, born March 1755, at New Haven, Conn. An officer in the American Army during the Revolution. Married Rhoda Collins, daughter of Charles Collins, and granddaughter of Rev. Timothy Collins, the 4th settled minister of Litchfield, Conn., March ——, 1780. Died at New Haven, Feb. ——,

1809, and was buried in the "New Burying Ground."
Rhoda Collins Pierrepont, died at Livonia, N.Y., 1845.
2. Robert Pierrepont, 2d son, born June 13, 1757, at New
Haven, Conn. Married Oct. 11, 1780 (his wife's birth-
day), Lois Collins, daughter of Charles Collins, and
grand daughter of Timothy Collins, (see Rhoda Collins
above), who was the great-grandson of John Collins of
Boston, who came from England in 1640, and died
March 29, 1670. Timothy Collins married Elizabeth
Hyde, the great-granddaughter of William Hyde, one
of the original proprietors of Norwich, who came to
America with the Rev. Thomas Hooker, (the first
minister of Hartford), in 1633. Timothy's mother
was Anna Leete, granddaughter of Gov. William
Leete.

This Lois Collins, who married Robert Pierrepont,
was born at Litchfield, Oct. 11, 1757, and was sister
to Rhoda Collins, married Evelyn Pierrepont, and to
Elizabeth Collins, married James Pierrepont. Robert removed with his wife and five daughters to Manchester, Vermont, about 1795, and resided there for
the remainder of his life. His wife Lois, died at
Manchester, Vt., May 5, 1826. He died at Plattsburgh, N. Y., where he had been visiting his daughter
Laura, (Mrs. Anson Sperry), August 16, 1835. He
and his wife are both buried at Manchester, Vt.
Original portraits of them are in the possession of
E. S. Isham, Chicago, Ill. Their children were:

(A.) Frances, born May 29, 1782, at Litchfield, South
Farms, Conn. Married Sept. 18, 1803, Richard
Skinner, afterwards Govenor of Vermont. She
died Aug. 29, 1843, buried at Manchester, Vermont.
The following are her children:
1. Susan P., born May 31, 1804, married May 18, 1831,
to Winslow C. Watson, of Port Kent, N. Y., son
of Elkanah Watson, a patriot of the Revolution
of 1776, and a descendant of Governor Edward
Winslow, of Massachusetts, and of the Earls of
De La Warre, in England. She died Jan. 26,
1845. Children living (1880,) are:
1. Winslow Charles Watson, Jr., born Jan. 19,

1832. Graduated at University of Vermont, in 1854. Admitted to the bar of the State of New York, 1861. Married, first, Mary A. Arnold, daughter of Silas Arnold, of Keeseville, Essex Co., N. Y. She died, childless, in 1862.

Married, second, Ella S. Barnes, of Addison, Vermont, Sept. 23, 1879. He was elected Judge and Surrogate of Clinton Co., N. Y., in 1875.

A son, Winslow Barnes Watson. Born Aug. 28, 1880, at Plattsburgh, N. Y.

2. Frances S. Watson, born Aug. 5, 1836, married H. N. Hewitt, of Keeseville, N. Y.

3. Mary Emily Watson. Born July 19, 1842, married Luther Whitney, of Keeseville, N. Y.

A daughter, Susan, was born, Feb. 9, 1881.

2. Frances, born Aug. 18, 1808, first wife of the above named Winslow C. Watson, was married to him May 28, 1824. She died April 26, 1829, at Manchester, Vt., leaving one child, Richard S. Watson, born April 21, 1829, married Cynthia Ferris, daughter of Hiram Ferris, of Chazy, Clinton Co., N. Y., Dec. 21, 1854. Their only child, Frances S. Watson, born Sept. 15, 1855, married in 1875, John Roy Lewis, of Brooklyn, N. Y. They have two children:

1. Winslow W.
2. Harry.

3. Timothy Collins Skinner, born at Manchester, Nov. 17, 1805, died March 1, 1806.

4. Hon. Mark Skinner, born Sept. 13, 1813. Graduated at Middlebury in 1833. Shortly afterwards he married, and removed to Chicago, Ill., which was then a village. He has resided there ever since, to the present year (1880.) His children:

1. Elizabeth.
2. Frances (Mrs. Willing.)
3. Frederika B.
4. Susan.
5. His oldest son, Richard, graduated at Yale Col-

lege in 1862, entered the United States army, and was placed on the staff of Gen. Hunter. Killed at the battle of Petersburgh, Va., in 1865, unmarried.

6. The only remaining son, Evelyn P., died, unmarried and a minor, at Chicago, Ill.

(B.) Nancy, born Oct. 24, 1784, at Litchfield, Conn., married June 21, 1801, Dr. Ezra Isham, of Colchester, Conn. He removed to Manchester, Vt., and lived there till his death. She died at Dunkirk, N. Y., 1868. Their children:

1. Pierpont Isham, born Aug. 5, 1802. Was for many years Judge Supreme Court of Vermont. Removed to Piermont, N. Y., from Bennington, Vt., in 18—. His wife was Samantha Swift, of Bennington, a daughter of Dr. Noah Swift. Their children:
   1. Edward Swift.
   2. Mary Adaline.
   3. Henry Pierpont.
2. Caroline, born Dec. 28, 1803, married June 1, 1836, to George Bradley. Their children:
   1. Eliza P.
   2. Ezra C.
3. Mary, born March 23, 1806, died Aug. 22, 1828, unmarried:
4. Jane, born July 27, 1810, died Sept. 1, 1810.
5. Edwin, born June 27, 1812, married Eliza ——. Their children:
   1. George Pierpont, born June 19, 1840.
6. John, born June 30, 1817, married ——. His children:
   1. Anna P., born June 20, 1856.

(C.) Esther, born May 14, 1787, married Calvin Sheldon, of Rupert, Vt., a graduate of Middlebury, Vt., and a lawyer. Settled at Manchester, Vt., where she died, 1833. Their children:

1. John C. Sheldon died unmarried.
2. Richard S. Sheldon. His children:
   1. David D., born 1839.
   2. Stephen C., born 1842.

3. Julia Sheldon, born 1815. Married Dr. John Darby, of Macon, Ga. Their children:
    1. John.
    2. Julia.
4. Christina Sheldon, born 1817, married Benjamin Richards. Their children:
    1. Benjamin.
    2. William.
5. Robert Sheldon died in infancy.

(D.) Laura, born Jan. 30, 1791, married Jan. 9, 1812, Anson J. Sperry, eldest son of Philo Sperry, of New Haven, Conn. He was a lawyer at Plattsburgh, N. Y., where he died and was buried. She died at New Haven, 1873, buried at Manchester, Vt. Their children:

1. Charles Sperry, born Nov. 15, 1812. An officer in the U. S. Navy. Died May 12, 1836, unmarried.
2. Elizabeth Sperry, born Oct. 22, 1815, married Gen. B. S. Roberts, U. S. Army, Sept. 18, 1836. He died in Washington, D. C., 1876. Their children, living:
    1. Benjamin K., in 1880, 1st Lieut. U. S. A.
    2. Evelyn P.
    3. Harris L., at West Point in 1880.
3. Pierpont Sperry, born Sept. 11, 1822, married March 17, 1846, died July 18, 185–. His children:
    1. Laura M., born Dec. 18, 1847.
    2. Louisa E., born June 8, 1849.
4. Anson Sperry, born Oct. 1, 1824, married Feb. 28, 1849. His children:
    1. Charles C., born April 21, 1851.
    2. Laura E., born May 16, 1855.
    3. Edwin A., } born Oct. 6, 1857.
    4. Evelyn P., }

Julia, (youngest daughter), born March 9, 1793, at Harwinton, Conn., married, first, Richard H. Warne, of Mayfield, N. Y. (1822). He was a graduate of Union College, (1816), and a lawyer by profession. Had one child, Henry, who died in infancy. Mr. Warne died at Manchester, Vt., in 1824. She married second, Dr. E. Marks, of Barhamville, near Columbia, S. C. He was a graduate of the New York Medical College, (1815), and principal of the South Carolina College for ladies at Barhamville, from 1821 to 1861. Living at Washington, D. C., in 1880. She died at Washington, D. C., June 21, 1878. Their children, (besides three who died in childhood), are:

1. Edwina Pierrepont Marks, born at Barhamville, S. C., Jan. 30, 1835, married Oct. 25, 1880, to Major Wm. N. Chamberlin, of Gibson, Penn. Now living at Washington, D. C.

2. Edward J. Marks, born at Barhamville, S. C., March 31, 1841. Educated at the Collegiate and Commercial Institute, (Gen. Wm. H. Russell, principal), of New Haven, Conn., (1854–1855), and at Jamaica Plain, near Boston, (1857). Entered Harvard College in 1858, and was there till August 1861, when the outbreak of the civil war recalled him to Carolina. Was Deputy Naval Officer of U. S. Customs, at Charleston, S. C., 1866–69, admitted to the New York bar, 1875. Is now, (1880), in the Surrogate's Court, Plattsburgh, N. Y.

3. James Pierrepont, born Jan, 4, 1761, at New Haven, Conn., married September 24, 1782, Elizabeth Collins, daughter of Charles Collins, of Litchfield, Conn. She was born at Litchfield, Sept. 25, 1755, and died at South Farms, Conn., July 28, 1815.

He married, second, Lucy Crossman, Dec. 16, 1817. She died in 1835. He had by her one son, Leonard Pierrepont, born Oct. 28, 1819.

James Pierrepont died at Litchfield in 1840. His children, by his wife Elizabeth, were:

(A.) Sherman Pierrepont, born June 29, 1783, at Litchfield, Conn., married Dec. 1, 1807, was drowned in Lake Erie, May 7, 1836. His children were:

1. George, born May 21, 1819, married April 20, 1840. Living in Bristol, Conn., in 1858.

2 Minerva, born Sept. 4, 1809, married Nov. 27, 1827, Sherman P. Woodward, of Watertown. Died Aug. 22, 1837, at Litchfield. Their children:

1. Rachel P., a graduate of Ft. Edward Institute, in 1857.

2. Minerva, P., born in 1836. married April, 1857, Garwood Judd, of Watertown. Living in Illinois, in 1858.

(B.) John Pierrepont, or (Pierpont,) born April 6, 1785, at Litchfield, Conn., married Sept. 23, 1810, died 1866. He was successively a lawyer, a merchant, and pastor of a Congregational church in Boston, Massachusetts, from 1819-45, afterwards in Troy, N. Y., and Medford, Massachusetts, till 1856. In 1861 he became Chaplain of a Massachusetts regiment, and soon after was appointed to a clerkship in Washington. He published "Airs of Palestine, and other Poems," and lectured extensively throughout the United States.

He was an abolitionist, and a temperance reformer. He was twice married; by his second wife he had no children. By his first wife he had:

1. William Alston, born July 11, 1811, at Litchfield, married, first, Mary C. Ridgway, of Syracuse, N. Y., second, Sarah Turelle, of Boston. Had one daughter, Mary L.

2. Mary E., born Sept. 18, 1812, at Newburyport, unmarried in 1857.

3. Juliette, born July 30, 1816, at Baltimore, married 1836, Junius S. Morgan, of Hartford, Conn. Their children:

   1. John Pierrepont, born April 17, 1837.
   2. Sarah Spencer, born Nov. 5, 1844.
   3. Junius Spencer, born April 6, 1846.
   4. Juliette P., born Dec. 24, 1847.

4. John, born Nov. 24, 1819, at Boston, Massachusetts, was in Savannah, Ga., in 1857.

5. James, born April 25, 1822, at Boston Massachusetts, married Mellicent Cowen, of Troy, Sept. 4, 1846. Their children:

   1. Mary, born Aug. 20, 1847.
   2. John, born Aug. 11, 1849.

6. Caroline Augusta, born Aug. 21, 1823, at Boston, married J. M. Boardman, of Macon, Ga. Their children:

   1. Arthur E.
   2. Maria F.
   3. Juliette M.
   4. Mellicent P.

5. Frederick M.
6. George L.
7. Henry H.

(C.) Elizabeth Pierrepont, born May 28, 1790, married Rev. J. Langdon. Their children:
1. Dr. Timothy Langdon, Naugatuck.
2. John Langdon.
3. James L. Langdon.
4. Elizabeth Langdon.

(D.) Abby Pierrepont, born Oct. 13, 1797, married Rev. J. Langdon. Their children:
1. David Langdon.
2. Sarah Langdon.

(E.) James Morris Pierrepont, born 1800, at Litchfield, Conn., married S. Harrison, died in 1839. Had one son, Robert Pierrepont.

(F.) James Pierrepont died in childhood.

(G.) Sarah B. Pierrepont, born 1787, died in childhood.

(H.) Sarah B. Pierrepont, born 1794, married —— Coggeshall, died at Brooklyn.

4. David Pierrepont,[1] born in New Haven, Conn., July 26, 1764, married Sarah Phelps, daughter of Edw. Phelps, of Litchfield, Conn., born Oct. 4, 1766. He died Feb. 1826. She died 1851. Their children:

(A.) David Pierrepont, born Dec. 19, 1788. Lived at Allen's Hill, Richmond, Ontario Co., N. Y. Died April 3, 1862, married Sally Palms, born May 21, 1791. Their children:
1. David A., lives at Allen's Hill, Ontario, N. Y. His children:
   1. David.
   2. Caroline.
2. Frances A., married Marcius Wilson (the historian), Vineland, N. J. Their children:
   1. Pierrepont.
   2. Caroline.
   3. Fannie.
   4. Robert P.

---

[1] I am indebted to L. L. Pierpont, Esq., of Ontario, New York, and Miss J. Pierpont, of Rutland, Vt., for facts relative to David Pierrepont.

3. Ogden E., Rochester, N. Y., has two children.
4. Caroline, married Geo. Townsend, has one child, Caroline E. Townsend.

(B.) Robert Pierrepont, Rutland, Vt., born May 4, 1791, died Sept. 23, 1864, married Abby Raymond. He was for many years Judge of the Circuit Court in Vermont. Their children (living):
1. Evelyn, married Miss Barret, has one child, Annie E.
2. Susan.
3. Julia.

(C.) Edward Pierrepont, born July 1, 1793, died Aug. 9, 1871, married Olive Blakeslee, born May 1, 1789. Their children:
1. George, Thomaston, Conn., has two daughters.
2. Andrew, Litchfield, Conn., has two daughters.
3. Edward, occupies his grandfather's old homestead in Litchfield. His children:
   1. Albert.
   2. Frederick.
   3. Nellie.
4. Charles. No issue.

(D.) Warren Pierrepont, born Aug. 7, 1795. Lived at West Bloomfield, N. Y., living in 1880, married Feb., 1823, Polly Blakeslee, born Aug. 6, 1796. Their children:
1. Julia E. Clemons, born Aug. 18, 1824. No children.
2. Sarah A. Barnard, born Feb. 17, 1827. Lives West Bloomfield, N. Y. Twice married. Has one daughter, Sarah.
3. Oliver A. Pierrepont, born March 14, 1829, died May 27, 1832.
4. S. Nelson Pierrepont, born Nov. 9, 1830, lives at Owasse, Michigan, has 3 children.
5. Robert Pierrepont, born March 25, 1837, lives at Blue Rapids, Kansas, has five children.
6. Mary A. Smith, born Feb. 4, 1840, lives at Meadville, Pa., has four children.

(E.) Sarah A. Pierrepont, born Aug. 21, 1797, died Bay City, Michigan, married —— Greene. One son, Pierrepont ——, and two daughters.

(F.) William Pierrepont, born Jan. 31, 1800, died Watertown, N. Y., 1859. His children:
1. Sabra Kellogg, Rochester, N. Y., three children:
   1. Harriet.
   2. Fannie.
   3. Robert.
2. Hester Colvin, Saratoga, N. Y., has two daughters.

(G.) Charles Pierrepont, born May 22, 1802, died Oct. 31,
1875, at Allen Hill, Ontario Co., N. Y. His children:
1. Lucius L., born March 17, 1835. Lives at Allen
   Hill, Ontario Co., N. Y. His children:
   1. Nettie N., born Aug. 9, 1860.
   2. Frank E., born Feb. 4, 1866.
2. John, born Jan. 1, 1828, lives at Allen Hill.

(H.) John Pierrepont, born Sept. 10, 1805, Vergennes, Vt.
Now, (1880), Chief Justice of the Supreme Court,
and Chancellor of Vermont. His children:
1. Henry V., has two sons.
2. Nellie.
3. Caroline S., married —— Cobb, has two sons.

(I.) Laura E. Pierrepont, born Sept. 12, 1802, died Bennington, Mich., March 16, 1878, married —— Bancroft. Her children:
1. David P., has two children.
2. Jane B. Decker, has a daughter.
3. Laura Pope.

Children of Evelyn Pierrepont and Rhoda Collins, his wife.

(A.) Evelyn Pierrepont, born at Litchfield, Conn., Dec. 2,
1790, eldest son, died (unmarried), at sea, during
the war of 1812, off the coast of Norway.

XXIV.

(B.) Hezekiah Beers Pierrepont, born at Litchfield, Conn.,
July 28, 1792, married May 29, 1814, at New Haven,
by Rev. Samuel Merwin, to Mary Mulloy, a daugh-
ter of Edward Mulloy, of New York. · He died at
Rochester, N. Y., in 1872, and was buried at Avon,
N. Y., where he had formerly been a minister.

(C.) James Pierrepont, born at New Haven, July 11, 1795,

killed in a duel at New Orleans, in 1823, was never married.

(D.) William Pierrepont, born at New Haven, Aug. 20, 1797, married in Bristol, Conn., Sophronia Frisbie, of Burlington, Conn. She died in 1860. He lived at "Pierrepont Place," near Wharton, Texas. His children were:

1. James.
2. Frances.
3. Frederick.

He married, second, Mrs. Austin, widow of the great Texas land owner. They had one son, John Austin Pierrepont.

William Pierrepont died in 1870, when on his way from home to the city of Houston.

(E.) Frederick Wolcott Pierrepont, born at New Haven, Aug. 17, 1802, married Hannah Eliza Becker, of Pittstown, N. Y., (at Lewiston,) N. Y., Oct. 30, 1825. He died at New Haven, May 5, 1877. His widow is still, (1880,) at New Haven. Their children:

1. Frederick Lorenzo, born Dec. 5, 1826, married Mary Ferguson, at Fair Haven, Nov. 29, 1857, served three years in the 15th Regiment, Conn. Volunteers. Living in New Haven, in 1880.

2. Frances Rebecca, born Nov. 17, 1828, married Elias Gilbert Martin, at New Haven, Nov. 22, 1860. He died Dec. 25, 1867, of consumption, contracted while in command of the "Racer," South Atlantic Blockading Squadron, having served in the United States Navy nearly four years. Buried in New Britain. She lives in New Haven, (1880).

3. Jesse Evelyn, born March 27, 1831, married Mary A. Turner, at Fair Haven, May 30, 1853. He was a member of Co. —, 27th Regt. Conn. Vols. Living in New Haven, (1880).

4. Joseph Collins, born Aug. 17, 1833, married Olive Bunnell, at Fair Haven, June 27, 1855, living in Westfield, Mass, (1880).

5. William Henry, born Oct. 22, 1836. A member of Co. "F" 7th Regt. Conn. Vols., served four

years, from private to captain in the 7th Regt. and as A. C. M. on the staff of Maj. Gen. Joseph R. Hawley. Living in Albany, (1880,) an invalid from wounds received in the army.

6. James Becker, born May 12, 1839, married Jane Payne, at New Britain, Conn., April 4, 1866. Living at New Britain, (1880).

7. Edwin Finne, born May 24, 1842. A member of Co. "F" 6th Regt. Conn. Vols. In a night attack on Ft. Wagner, Charleston, S. C., was wounded in three places, from which he never recovered. Died at sea, (while on a voyage for his health), July 28, 1867.

8. John, born Aug. 16, 1845, married Emma A. Akerman, at Fair Haven, Jan. 4, 1866. Was a member of Co. "K" 10th Regt. Conn. Vols. Discharged before expiration of term; very severely wounded. Living at Mormon Island, Cal. (1880.)

(F.) Lorenzo Pierrepont, born at New Haven, March 23, 1805, was an officer in the U. S. Navy, and died in the Florida war, on board the "Cyane."

(G.) Sophia H. Pierrepont, born March 9, 1785, at Litchfield, Conn., married, Nov., 1801, Jacob Goodsell, of New Haven, where she died. Their children:

1. Alfred C., born Aug. 30, 1803, married Sarah Ludington. Their children:
   1. Alfred.
   2. Sarah.
   3. Samuel.
   4. Almira.
   5. Willis.

2. Samuel M., born Feb. 11, 1805, died Sept. 13, 1829, unmarried.

3. Louisa H., born Nov. 24, 1807, married Jesse J. Ball. Living at Fair Haven in 1880. Their children:
   1. Adaline.
   2. Henry.

4. Evelyn P., born May 11, 1810, married Eliza Talmadge. Their children:
   1. Evelyn.
   2. Ann.

3. Jeannette.
5. Charlotte A., born Jan. 22, 1812, married Volney
    Pierce. Their children:
    1. Sarah.
    2. Sophia.
    3. John.
    4. George.
6. Sarah M., born Dec. 20, 1813, died Jan. 27, 1814.
7. Frances A., born Oct. 15, 1814, died Sept. 20, 1815.
8. James H., born Jan. 24, 1816, married, first, Reumah
    Mallory, second, Mary Stevens. Their Children:
    1. Reumah.
    2. Mary.
    3. Ann G.
    4. Bessie.
    5. Burdette.
9. George W., born March 13, 1818, married Abigail
    Nettleton. Their children:
    1. Frances.
    2. Georgiana.
    3. Josephine.
    4. George.
10. John D., born Dec. 13, 1820, married Emeline Tur-
    ner. Their children:
    1. Emma.
    2. Elizabeth.
    3. Frances.
    4. George.
11. Willis J., born April 3, 1824. Married Ann Good-
    win. One child: Grace D.

(H.) Philena Pierrepont, born Jan. 29, 1787, at Litchfield.
    Married Hezekiah Davenport, of New Haven, where
    she died. Their children:
1. Paulina, married —— Parker,
2. James P., settled in South America.
3. John, married, lives at Northford, Conn.
4. Henrietta, married George Walker. Living in New
    York in 1857.
5. Nancy, married Leonard Bond. Living in Brooklyn
    in 1857.

6. Augusta, married —— Currier, of Chester. Was a
widow, living in New Haven in 1857.
7. Frances, married Edward Hayes. Living in New
York in 1857.
8. Samuel, married —— ——, living in California in
1857.
(I.) Anna Sherman Pierrepont, born Jan. 3, 1789, at Litchfield. Married Richard James. Lived in Rochester in 1857. Went to Wisconsin, where she died
in 1874. Their children:
1. Frances, married Edw. Price, of Avon Springs, N. Y.
2. Eliza, married Lorraine Bradley, Davenport, Iowa.
3. Mary, married Wm. Holman, of Cleveland, Ohio.
4. Elizabeth, married —— Bates, of Iowa. Living in
1857.
(K.) Frances Edwards Pierrepont,[1] born at Fair Haven,
Conn., Oct. 15, 1800, married Luther R. Laselle,
of Troy, N. Y., where she is living in 1880. She
was married July 5, 1824, by Rev. Aaron Lane, at
Phelps, Ontario Co., N. Y. Mr. Laselle was born
at Lanesborough, Mass., July 28, 1798. Their
children:
1. Elias James, born at Lyons, N. Y., April 1, 1825,
lives at Dunnville, Ontario, Canada, is married
and has one daughter. His two grandsons live
in Rochester, N. Y. Their name is Hawley.
2. Henry Edwards, born at Rochester, N. Y., Nov. 9,
1827, married Sarah Atsale. She is dead. He
died at Panama, Central America, Nov. 9, 1858.
They had a son and a daughter.
3. Lydia R., born at Brunswick, N. Y., March 15, 1830.
4. Frances S., born at Troy, N. Y., Sept. 8, 1832.
5. Mary G., born at Troy, N. Y., Jan. 29, 1835, married Charles Rogers. He is dead. She has a
daughter.
(L.) Elizabeth Pierrepont, born April 23, 1807, living in
1880, married Wm. McCoy, of Rochester, N. Y.
Their Children:

---

[1] To this lady, who has furnished me much valuable information in her own hand-
writing at the advanced age of 80 years, I owe many facts incorporated in this abstract of
descent.

1. Evelyn P.

2. Anna M., married Dr. Northrop, of Rochester.

3. Emeline, married James French, Buffalo, N. Y.

Children of Hezekiah Beers Pierpont, and Mary his wife.

1. Jane Pierrepont, died aged 18, unmarried.

2. Julia Anne Pierrepont, died aged 17, unmarried.

XXV.

3. James Pierrepont, eldest son, born in Pittsford, near
Rochester, N. Y., July 28, 1819, married Oct. 5,
1852, Maria Cushman Dibble. She was born June
18, 1832, the daughter of Sheldon Dibble, a mission-
ary, originally from Auburn, N. Y. She was a relative of Judge Cushman, of Troy, N. Y., and died
Nov. 18, 1862.

Mr. Pierrepont is the undoubted representative of
Sir George Pierrepont, of Holme Pierrepont, who
died in 1564. (See *ante.*)

He graduated at Hamilton College, New York, in
1849, and in Auburn Theological Seminary, in 1852,
was ordained to the ministry the same year. He resides in San Francisco, Cal., where he is in charge of
the Chapel to the Sailor's Home. His children are:

1. Maria G., born in Placerville, El Dorado Co., California, May 27, 1854.

2. Mary L., born in Sacramento City, California, June
22, 1856.

3. Clara S., born in Healdsburgh, Sonora Co., Cal.,
May 13, 1859.

---

4. Henry Sydney Pierrepont, resides at Two Rivers, Wisconsin, (after his brother James, he will represent
the family), was born March 3, 1823, at Rochester,
N. Y., married Lydia A. Gardner, of Syracuse, N.
Y., at Ottawa, Illinois, Oct. 14, 1852. Their children:

1. Julia, born in La Salle, Ill., March 16, 1854.

2. Caroline, born at Two Rivers, Wis., Aug. 17, 1857.

3. Henry Edward, born at Two Rivers, Wis., April 16,
1862.

4. Jane Emma, born at Green Bay, Wis., Oct. 29, 1867.

www.ingramcontent.com/pod-product-compliance
Lightning Source LLC
Chambersburg PA
CBHW071344290326
41933CB00040B/2278